MICAH'S SECOND COMING

PURPLE VIXEN

Fulton Books
Meadville, PA

Published by Fulton Books 2024

ISBN 979-8-88982-534-0 (paperback)
ISBN 979-8-88982-535-7 (digital)

Printed in the United States of America

INTRODUCTION

Hard rain starts to pour,
My Dark Mind is at war.
Every Dream Killer is at the show, waiting for the darkness to grow.
My Closed Heart is at play, while
Dreaming of you is hard to bear,
Remembering you isn't fair.
Farewell my Friend, this is true
seeing your Heavenly eyes is making me Blue.
Irresistible Lover, your Love Games drains my soul, loving you has
taken its toll,
but as of yet My Secret Lover will never be told.
As I slip out of my own mind, Sneaky Pink and Spicy Red is ready to
help me to clear my head,
Little Big Red with a smile so bright, clears out the darkness with his
shiny light.
Don't Block your Blessings because My 4 Protectors are near, I will
never have anything to fear.
Little Man brings me Positive Vibes while my First keeps me alive.
Big Sister is here to make you smile with My Sweet Angel will always
be mine.
My gray Clouds are gone,
replaced by love for My King and Queen that lives all above.

HARD RAIN

Watching the rain fall, hearing the thunder that shakes the skies.
Everything is dark and cloudy, hiding the sun that wants to break
through.
The storm is heavy, wind blowing so hard that it can knock you
down to the ground as you beg the wind to let you breathe:
the hardness of life will bury you alive so it seems.
The harder the rain falls, the deeper the ocean can drown you,
with life issues is how you learn to break through never let the storm
overpower your thoughts, hope or dreams.
There's always a reason for the wind to blow you down either with
depression, heartbreak, misery, or loneliness.
You never give into the storm, never let it control anything in your
life.
Take the power from the Storm,
Take the Thunder and Lighting, wield the power and make it your
own power and only your Power, turn it into your
Blessing, Love, Peace, Joy, and Happiness.
Beat the Storm that tried to Bury you alive and Rise above it!

Backstory

I wrote this poem because sometimes when it rains, it pours so
to speak. Sometimes life can be unbearable to deal with, but when
you rise up against the situation, you can change it or at least try to
turn things around.

Don't let the world beat you down; show that you can make a
difference.

My Dark Mind

The vision in my head plays with me, telling me all the bad things that's in my head are true. Why don't people notice me? because you're not important, you're not one of them, you're not Beautiful, you're ugly and fat, you're not worthy of love . Why do I feel this way? Because you're not a good person, you're useless to the world. Why is everyone against me? There's nothing you can offer to the world, no one wants you around. These are my thoughts that lingers in my mind – My dark secret that I keep to myself. This dark cloud is heavy, and it is suffocating my mind that I can't breathe and see no light – the voices are strong and it's draining all my energy that I have.

The voices in my head tells me that I'm not good enough to be in this world, I'm useless, worthless, undesirable, no one will ever love me, and I will be alone for the rest of life.

These are the thoughts that clouds my mind saying that I will never be nothing but a bother to the people that's in this world and that I'm better off in death.

My Dark Mind is the hell that I must live with until my light comes back to me but right now, I am haunted by memories that will play in my head in the deep darkness of my mind and thoughts.

Memories of people leaving me alone to face my demons in the darkness.

I must confess that I will not be down for long, I will find my light once again. Until that day comes I will sit in the corner and pray that my darkness will not take over.

This is my Dark Mind.

Back Story

This right here was tough for me to write, because at this time in my life I was very depressed and couldn't find a way out of this rut. Everything was so heavy in my heart and my life was just too much for me to take. I was in a very dark place until I realized that I am good enough to be here and found the light I was looking f or. I became a stronger and healthier person, because I wrote this poem to get the negative thinking out of my head. This poem helped me think more clearly and helped me step out of the darkness that covered my light, in some way more than you know some people need help in stepping out of their darkness that's been covering their light.

DREAM KILLERS

In this time or the next, there's always someone trying to destroy or
distain a person from reaching their goals in life.
People always try to bring you down.
They will make you second guess everything you do, you start to
doubt your abilities, in making bad decisions or mistakes.
You don't know what to do, you don't know how to feel or act in
trying to decide on the next move you should take.
They work on your mind, getting you confused by playing games as
if you're not good enough to do anything or even to be success-
ful in the life path you're taking.
They will drain your positive energy and replace it with negative
thoughts of giving up.
They are called Dream Killers who came into your life.
If you have Dream Killers, pay them no mind they're the one run-
ning out of time.

Backstory

I wrote this poem because in life, things and people change in
some shape or form. Everyone has someone in their life who always
finds a way to try and distract you from pursuing your goals. They
feel if they didn't or couldn't succeed in life, they will make you feel
the same way. But the thing is, they don't have your determination
or the drive to get where they want to go. Don't let them turn you
into them; keep going and have faith within yourself that what you're
trying to accomplish will come to you in folds.

Keep moving!

Closed Heart

I feel the heat of Love and Passion, it controls everything within me.

My eyes are filled with joy and happiness, everything that I touch turns into beautiful colors that express themselves to live and to be Loved.

The flowers, trees, grass and everything in between, the world will not survive if Love is taken for grated.

Without more laughter or joy it will cause great damage to a heart that gave so much.

If you close your heart, you're letting coldness settle in and inviting bitterness to take over where Love once lived.

A closed heart is a dead person walking around spreading Hate to the souls of the people they once knew.

Don't Close your heart, it may seem easy to do,

Giving up on things and people that you gotten used to, don't give into the sadness and bitterness that will lead you to closing off the world.

Let the tears flow the pain and hurt away.

Don't shut off, don't give in to the depression and misery that plays with your mind within display.

Don't give into the pressure of other people's opinion on how you live your life.

Don't every close your heart,

Live your life!

Backstory

This poem is about depression and how some people feel when they are alone—overthinking everything they are going through.

Some think that once something goes bad, their whole life is doomed, but in truth, it's not. At that time, it wasn't right for you, and maybe if you try again, it will work out. Just because the day was weird doesn't mean you failed; it was just not your time, but it will be soon.

DREAMING OF YOU

I close my eyes at night
the colorful world comes to play in my mind
all the places that I hope to see is right there that I can touch
My mind pictures your face and voice to make a clear image of you.
I Dream of You when I'm happy or sad.
You bring me so much peace and joy when you walk in my dream
       that I have created just to keep you in mind's eye.
The way we talk always makes me feel that you are here with me
       and making my frown disappear as you give me advice on life
       lessons.
I wish I could stay in this fantasyland with you and all my family that
       passed away.
Seeing you smile and laugh again, but I know that I can always see
       you in my mind's eye of many Dreams to come.
I shall hold you in my heart and remember everything that you had
       told me,
I Dream of you when I'm happy or sad,
you hug me and say that everything will be okay.
I will Dream of you every day until we meet again. I Love you
Grandma hugs

Backstory

This poem is dedicated to my grandmother. One day, I will see her again. Hugs and kisses.

REMEMBERING YOU

I sit and smile as memories of you flash in my mind, the way that you
    talk, walk, smile, and laugh.
The feeling is strange, not having you around, but I know that you
    are still with me in spirit.
When I feel so alone, I look into the heavens and see that you are
    making a way for me to see clearly.
The tears that roll down my face are not of sadness but of joy, cele-
    bration of the life that you lived and shared.
Remembering you brings joy to my heart and helps ease the pain of
    missing you.
Remembering you, my Big Brother, my Protector, and now my
    Angel.
So farewell for now, I will see you again so fly high to heavens and
    shine as Brightly as the Sun.

Backstory

I wrote this because my uncle passed away, and my mother
asked me to write a poem for her, and this is what I wrote for her to
remember her brother, protector, and her angel.

I dedicate this poem to him.

Farewell, My Friend

I never realized how much time I wasted on you in caring and loving
    only you
You never showed me any type of love in return and you never will
    as time goes on.
I never let it bother me before until one night when you made a
    choice that you never wanted or needed me in your life.
I've always known how you felt, I just gave you those chances that
    you didn't deserve,
but I did anyway because I cared enough to give you
those chances.
I hold no hard feelings or grudges.
I hope that you are Blessed in every way, shape, or form.
I have a lot of walls built up around myself because of the lessons I've
    learned over the years.
Never give yourself completely to one person, they will always disap-
    point you in return.
I'm letting go of All the hurt and pain that you have caused me.
I let this happen, I waited too long to really see the damage that you
    were causing me for the love that you will never show.
So now that I'm free without worry, I'm happy with myself and
    maybe one day,
I will find someone who will *love* me for me.
I'm choosing myself above everything and not letting no one take my
    Power away from me again,
it's been a long time coming and it feels *amazing*.
The *love* that I have for myself is *priceless*—
I feel better when you're not here, I can breathe in fresh air all around.

I do feel Sorrow but not enough to keep dealing with you coming,
    going in and out of my life.
I wanted to be with you and only you, instead you chose to be with
    everyone else.
You chose peasants over Thee Queen.
I will never submit to you; you weren't worthy of me because we were
    on different levels of life.
Trust and believe I'm not
putting all the blame on you. I'm woman enough to take some
    accountability for my actions.
It took too long, now I'm moving forward without you and keeping
    my eyes open with my mind clear. So Farewell my Friend, it was
    nice knowing you.

Backstory

This poem is about breaking free from a person who you were not meant to be with; this person was seasonal. I shouldn't have stayed around as long he/she did because now they have gotten used to me being there while they're coming and going, knowing that I would always let them back in. But now you understand your worth as a man or woman; you don't have to let them in no more. You're free to get out into the world and live your life without regret.

Go ahead, break those chains and love yourself more than ever before.

Heavenly Eyes

I look into your eyes and I can see Heaven's sparkle inside,
all the colors of your soul reveal your stories that you haven't told.
The hurt,pain,love,kindness,joy,happiness and peace that you hold
in your heart.
Your eyes tell the story that your mind keeps secret, holding your
deepest feelings that are hidden from the world.
Your eyes keep me memorized with every glance that you give.
The pureness in your smile makes your eyes beam with joy.
Heavenly Eyes I sit and look for the stories that you're willing to
share.
giving me hope that one day I'll be able to stare into your eyes with
peace and calmness that I can feel complete and will not share.
Heavenly Eyes, I'm lost in your glaze, willing to give you anything to
be amazed.
The sparkle in your eyes sets a fire into my soul, just tell me with
your eyes what should be told. Your lips curl up into a smile,
making me wonder why I feel so alive.
Heavenly Eyes you're my heart, thank you so much even though
we're far apart.
Heavenly Eyes this much is true, I'll see you again because I only
have love for you.

Backstory

This poem is about a love that was good and pure and that these
two just love one another to the very end. He remembers his love by
her eyes being so beautiful; that's only one reason why he fell for her
like he did.

He felt peace and love every time he looked into her eyes, and he was in heaven with her.

When you find that kind of love, you will know that he/she will have your heavenly eyes.

BLUE

Blue is the color of calm, cool breeze, the ocean and sky.
Blue is the serene paradise full of joy, peace and happiness
Blue is the color of sadness, lost, confused and hopeless.
Blue is hurt, pain and disappointment that will kill your soul.
For me, these are my feelings that I had ever since you left this world
far too soon.
I can't talk or feel happiness because you're not here to share the joys
of everyday life.
To breathe the same air or see what the future may have held for you.
But as I cry of letting you go, for the freedom of your soul to join the
Angels in the sky above.
Blue has changed the way I see things, facing the world with more
confidence, holding my head high, looking for your smile to
brighten my day even though that will not happen today.
One day I will, so here's to you and your color Blue.
Thanks for the smiles, laughter and the honor of loving you; now
that's my type of Blue.

Backstory

I wrote this poem for all the people who miss someone they love. I like the ocean that seems to calm the soul when you're feeling a little down and out. So hopefully, this poem will bring you peace within yourself.

IRRESISTIBLE LOVER

Sitting here alone that's nothing new, my head in the clouds thinking
about you.
No matter the season that comes and goes you're always on my mind.
I miss your face, Oh how I miss your face, you have that million-dol-
lar smile that can never be replaced.
My heart skips a beat when I hear your name, no one has ever been
able to treat me the same,
with your gentle hand that held me so tight, no one else can ever get
that right.
Irresistible Love, you should be ashamed of how you treat us women
like a game.
Your strategy is key in pleasing and teasing me that I cannot explain.
You're smart and charming, that's enough to be alarming.
Irresistible Lover, you're dishonest, unkind and never true one of
these days you'll be blue.
Your charms will fade in your little escapade.
You will look back on the frail trail knowing your game is up from
another tragic derailment failure of love.
So Irresistible Lover, this much is true I'm really not feeling you.

Backstory

The reason why I wrote this poem is because I have been think-
ing about someone I used to care for deeply, and he broke my heart
with his lies and false promises, but I have learned to move forward
without him being in my life. So if you ever felt this way, hopefully
when you read this, it will bring a smile to your face.

LOVE GAMES

You say that you Love me, then you leave me again,
Stop playing these Love Games where I never win.
I thought when I met you, your feelings were true
You said that you Loved me, if only I knew,
So if you get bored, depressed, or down, don't come running to me
because I won't be around.
Love is not a game when the winner is you,
Love's an Emotion shared between two

Backstory

This poem is about when you fall for the wrong person, thinking that they have feelings for you, and they are just playing with your heart, never willing to give themselves to you as much as you give to them.

Don't play yourself in giving your all to someone who will not do the same for you.

SECRET DREAM LOVER

You're so sweet and gentle, I feel so complete being swept off my feet.
While all your attention is focused on me, I appreciate the kindness
that you have been giving me.
Your gentle touch is so very new, I never knew my body could move
with you, holding me so close all through the night, keeping
me warm and snuggle tight, just being with you feels so right.
Your kisses smooth like milk, the touch of your lips feels like silk, the
smell of your scent drives me wild, I can't wait to see you in a
little while.
Caressing your body brings fire to my eyes, in taking everything you
have without any disguise.
Secret Dream Lover come see me tonight, bring me pleasure all
through the night. You're the best I've ever known, canceling
the rest to unknown.
Secret Dream Lover, this much is true, I'm falling for you. I opened
my eyes to watch the darkness disappear, realizing that I only
dreamt you were here.

Backstory

Well, this poem came from dream that many of us have, of the
person that we sometimes we cannot have or for someone we know
but never got a chance to tell them in our waking state of mind, so
this is just a love note that we keep to ourselves for our own special
time with the person in our dreams.

Sneaky Pink

Cold as Ice, Cool like the Breeze
This little lady is never a tease.
The role she plays will soothe your soul,
once you're hooked, it should never be told.
Don't play no games because you will lose
Sneaky Pink always wins in everything she choose.
She will make all your dreams come true, but will also leave you broken and confused.
Through her life many men had tried to play her like a fool, but it's them that has been fooled.
She will leave her print, making them break their own rules.
She's bright, smart and loveable as she can be, if you do her wrong she will leave you like a fallen tree.
Sneaky Pink is very unique; her heart is a sweet treat.

Backstory

This poem is about a woman who has been handed a hard lesson in love; she has been through so much, but she learns how to play the games of love.

This is a lesson to not play with people's hearts and emotions because you never know when the tables will turn.

SPICY RED

Hot as fire, warm as the red sea, some men would like her cup of tea.
The wind in her hair, the smell of her scent
will drive any man mad to represent.
The strength of her mind and body will catch you by surprise, the
spirit of her heart will haunt your soul.
She's wild at heart, playful as a child, but she's all woman that will be
worth your while.
Spicy Red is her name, she's very hard to handle and will never be
tamed.
Whenever she comes around, she's turning every man's head, while
staring at her from head to toe wondering where she may go?
Her heart is pure, with a smile that's golden,the skies open up with-
out withholdings.
She graces the land I love with a voice so sweet and innocent, while
holding the peace within her.
She'll make you wonder where she has been, hiding in the shadows
with beauty so striking that it got all the men liking.
Spicy Red is her name, I'm telling you now she plays no games.

Backstory

This poem is about a woman who can turn heads when she walks or talks. She's proud of the woman that she became and makes every man notice her as she moves through the street. She's not afraid to speak up for herself and let her voice be heard. She's a queen that can make anyone bow to her feet.

Are you a Spicy Red?

LITTLE BIG RED

Little Big Red is cool and laid-back, never takes life too seriously, just
  chill as he moves through the night.
The shadow that follows him around is a glowing light that makes
  him shine so bright.
The Red shows his Love for life and passion in his heart, no stressing
  over little things that might kill someone else in their own right,
Little Big Red has this glam about him, his smile and laughter just
  so right.
He's one person on this
Beautiful Land that will make everyone feel out of sight,
His voice is strong and Lean, but he's never mean, he's gentle as giant
But very protective as a Bear, trust and believe he really does care.
He's a kind man, that's the thing—he's always ready to battle in the
  ring.
Little Big Red is trusting and true, this is the reason why I Love you.

Backstory

This poem is about someone who's the nicest person you ever
want to meet; it could be someone you know for a long time or short.

But there's really no story for this one, just the love of a mother
has for her son. His personality and charm speak for themselves. If
your son or daughter makes your heart feel joy and happiness, I ded-
icate this poem to you and them.

Don't Block your Blessings

Your dream comes true with hard work that you put forth,
Now you can see your progress in many ways that you didn't know
were called *blessing*.
Blessings come in different ways that you could never imagine.
The air is more fresh with ideas that come to you so easily like crash-
ing waves on the ocean floor.
You can feel all the positive vibes you never felt before, roadblocks
removed
When the door was once closed another shall open with opportuni-
ties galore.
once was closed to you will welcome you with open arms.
When you let go of all the negativity that held you back and open
your mind and heart, things turn
around in ways you never thought that would happen.
Blessings will come your way once you let the
negative go and feel the positive flow throw your body,
the feeling of lightness when your mood changes,
you smile more, you see things differently.
Blessings are welcoming the new and washing away the old.
You start to love yourself again having the sun shining so brightly;
fading away the darkness.

Backstory

This poem is about when you have negative thoughts that are
blocking the good things for yourself; meaning the darkness in your

head is blocking what path you should take, but once you clear your head, things start to turn around. Positive thinking is good for you to have. Block out the negative, take in the positive.

MY 4 PROTECTORS

My 4 Protectors that's Big and True,
They Always have my back, and Everybody knew.
Their style is smart, cutting and smooth no one had it
like these dudes.
In the sky, with high standards in the lead flowing like the Gods
    indeed.
I never fear no *man* on this Earth, because
My 4 Protectors are always first.
Green, Red,
Blue, and Gold
My 4 Protectors will never be untold.
They have my back, front and my side—As long as they are here, I
    know that I will Survive
My 4 Protectors

Backstory

This poem is about growing up with a family that will protect you and always be there when you need them, never leaving you alone.

When you need a helping hand, you can always call a family member or friend.

Little Man

I've noticed a kind, gentle Soul for a young man that's not that old,
Big Ole smiles so happily and charming, that's so alarming.
When he's down, it's never for good; he bounces right back as he
should.
The joy in his eyes that sparkle and shine, that's why I'm glad this
little big guy is mine.
His heart is golden; his soul is pure; he's my guiding light to the
future unsure.
This little man makes my heart melt with his sweet smile from
heaven sent.
His personality is so new and bright that nothing is far out of sight.
When he's more mature, this much is true, he will never feel blue.
With cuddly hugs and kisses, this young man will never go missing;
he spreads his joy around to heal all that is hurting.
Maybe when he gets older, he will be a little flirty.
Right now he's young and still
learning that he can be whomever he chooses.

Backstory

This poem is about all the young men who have chosen to change the world as much as they can, trying to make a difference in others' lives. Firstborn young men always try to stand out and be something more than the people see, trying to make history. So this poem is for you; thanks for being you.

POSITIVE VIBES

Nothing in the world can stop you from moving.
You find your groove and tunes to make you move to the beat in the
world you created.
You find your strive to stay alive in this world we live in, shaking and
baking to the music in your head.
You have the flow that you show nothing's going to bring you down,
while dancing across town.
Your Positive drive is on a high, you're shaking up the world with
every step you make shows the world it's a piece of cake.
People are starting to feel your natural glow as your vibes start to
flow.
Moving and grooving to your own beat and sound, "Come On,
Positive Vibes, Let's Get Down"
Let's kick in this crazy drive.
Your prayers will come your way, just keep going and have a Positive
Day.

Backstory

This poem is about thinking differently and making changes in your lifestyle, smiling more, being happy and blessed. Not every day is going to be good, no mistake there, but if you just try to be you, then everything will be okay, therefore I wrote a poem feeling positive in doing things that will one day make someone smile.

I think that everyone can benefit from this poem. When you feel good, you smile more, you get in the groove to your own beat.

Positive vibe spreads joy and happiness.

MY FIRST

The first time I saw your face, I knew you had a place,
that big ole smile so pretty and sweet, that made my heart melt and
    it was unique.
Your first steps and words rang in my ear.
I knew from that moment I would always be near.
Times when you got in trouble, you ran up to me with fear, somehow
    knowing I will be here.
The moment you arrived, the sky was bright and in the moonlight
    that was so clear.
When I saw God's hand
touch your ear,
You're a blessing in the truest form, shall no harm come to you my
    sweet child.
From then to now you've grown up so fast, you turned sixteen and
    that's a blaste.
You were my first this much is true, now I turn to you wishing great
    joy and happiness for you.
You're a true blessing I must say, bringing me some laughter and
    some tears but you were My First and I Love You my dear.
You're my first but never last.

Backstory

This poem is about having your first child or grandchild, the
feeling that you have and the love that you shared. Over the years
you have watched them grow up and how much they have their own
personality and charm. You still see them as babies while you hold
them close in your arms. Your first and never your last.

MY BIG SISTER

I have someone that's precious to my heart, even though we live so
    far apart.
She's beautiful, kind, smart and generous, no one comes close to my
    first Best Friend.
We can talk for hours on end never needing to pretend,
her heart is full of Love that spreads to others from here to above.
I know this woman well through and through because she's my Big
    Sister, that is the truth.
With fairness and joy in heart is all I've ever known.
Thank you so much for being with me, now let's go sit underneath
    an apple tree to laugh and cry share our joy.
I will love you to the moon and back for eternity.

Backstory

I wrote this poem because we all have a sibling who is our very first best friend. Could be a sister, brother, or first cousin.

This is about having someone who's always there for you to cheer up and to show that they love you no matter what, and my first best friend is and always my big sister.

My Sweet Angel

There's a baby that is just so full of pure joy and a gift,
She's smart and cute. She's just a hoot.
With a dimple on one side of her cheek, yeah okay she's such treat,
her eyes are dark brown and
mysterious, but you can't never be down or blue when she's in the
  same room with you.
She's a gift from an angel above,
she just has so much love to give.
Her face is his, but her attitude is her own,
that's one thing everyone knows to be true.
She's a gift from an angel that lives in the sky that looks down with
  pride that he created this sweet child of mine.
Her smile and laughter are a sign that she will have a very bright
  future ahead of her,
giving praise to her is so simple that it brings tears to your eyes.

Backstory

All the people who have a very special person—either daughter, granddaughter, sister, or nieces. They are your sunshine when you're feeling sad, and they always find a way to make you smile and feel good no matter how your day went or is going. You're just happy that you have them in your life.

CLOUDS

Looking up at the clouds, oh how they make beautiful designs,
Painting a perfect picture to amaze the people standing outside.
They put on a show for you to watch how they can glow.
Beautiful colors of all shapes and sizes are so unique without ever
　　disguising with pure joy and fun.
When the clouds get dark with the threat of rain with all the broken
　　hearts that's in pain,
as the sun comes out to shine once more, for the tears that dropped
　　can be absurd.
The clouds dance to entertain people who are staring at the skies,
　　showing off their colors to dazzle and razzle as we peek at the
　　Clouds.

The story behind this poem

I look outside and just stare at the clouds that make all kinds
of pictures, moving like waves in the sky. I just love the colors and
shapes they make, love the clouds.

MY KING AND QUEEN

All my life I always knew that I had a King and Queen in my present,
I was born from the strength of strong men and women in my
bloodline. Their voices ring in my ear saying I am a Queen from
generations to come smart, classy, sassy, elegant, smooth and
sexy the best of the Best.

My King and Queen glance throw the crowd, and everyone turns to
bow their heads in respect,

As they step gracefully to their throne, they turn and nod their head
to their children not too far behind, their 4 Princes and their 2
Princesses. The Royal family has arrived, they are walking tall,
shoulders back and head high.

Staring ahead at their KING and QUEEN looking so proud at the
men and women walking down.

My King and Queen have done their job raising their children to fly
high to touch the skies, as they retire from their Throne saying
there's no place like home to welcome them with open arms .

My KING and QUEEN will always be the reason I am who I am,
never giving up on the people that have ruled before I, this is the
time to take our place on the Throne that will not be replaced.

Thank you for your blessings, love and respect.

Back-story

This poem is about parents, how over the years they have taken care
of us to understand life and the trials of the world. They were
our first teachers in this world, they called us their little prince
and princess, so we all feel special in some ways.

Now they look at us with pride and as we are grown and doing the same thing they have done for us, our King's and Queen's will always be within us.

INTRODUCTION

The Rhythm of time brings us here
The Journey was long we're almost near, you suppose to Serve
and Protect you got confused and lines were blurred;
Don't act like You Don't Care about the consequences of your actions,
     falling in the trap with all its repercussions.
Leave the N-Word
behind, it has passed its time, begin Tainted with
Your Decision(s) has you Changing Feelings while standing in a dif-
     ferent line.
Since you Left us
behind to Escape the killing of Sandlot in your mind,
I'm home looking at the Picture in the Frame, wondering will it ever
     be the same.
Both Sides of the Coin have been tossed;
it seems to me I might have lost.
I will take my leave, because Loving Myself is all I need.
Living in my own DreamLand, floating in the wide ocean span,
     swimming like a Mermaid without a plan,
I will Just Breath and Take this Day with ease, with The HourGlass
     slowly pouring Her Secrets out to soar around the Infinite Love
     that left her here,
circling around The Universe trying to live free and clear, The Water
     Fountain is drying up
hopefully you have a full cup. Changing things
never goes fast, beating you down with all the nasty and dirty trash
     that you dug around to just explore the world that wasn't yours.
Wishing on a Star to take you far away from the misery of people that
     just don't play.

But Loving You is what I have to steer myself away from, your falling
        fears and shaking from all your tears.
Karma has played her role in the failing
issues that are being exposed, Saying You're Sorry
Sometimes Isn't Enough, while you turn away and repeat the same
        History that brought you here
without mystery. Your Damaged Heart has failed
you again because you're missing your Beautiful
Queen that you once held so dear, fearing that you'll never see her
        again.
Leave the Purple Roses and call it the day
because there's nothing more for you to say. You
tried your damness to clear up the mess you made, start cleaning up
        your own backyard then you will see that
people you thought loved you will leave you be.
You will stand strong, take a deep breath and Just Breathe.

Rhythm

Close your eyes, take a deep breath, changing your energy with one quick breath.

Listening to your heartbeat makes a smooth rhythm to the melody as it creeps inside your bones.

Listening to this groove of time beating at your insides to come alive, blood starts to flood your veins, dripping to the sound playing a beat to feel the heat, shaking your shoulders to the music that you created. Moving your body to this crazy sound that got you moving all around, the rhythm is all in your head. Your Soul starts to come alive feeling the vibration coming along inside, snapping your fingers, to the beat hitting you with everything that is vibrating the streets.

Ease your mind, heart and soul, let the music take control. The Rhythm is taking the lead, your body is so relieved, flowing around with this funky sound, feeling good in your neighborhood, breaking it down to this marvels sound, can you feel it? Yeah break it down, soothe the mind, be kind to all as this music fills you up and never lets you down.
Feel the Rhythm

BackStory

When you are just sitting down relaxing and then you get a melody in your head, you just start to move. Feels good to let go and your body loses control to the music that plays in your head. Yeah that's what I'm talking about, feel the motion, dance around like no one is looking. This is why I wrote this poem Love listening to a good song that moves me. So get up move that body and have fun.

THE JOURNEY

All stories start off Rocky, but that's only if you let it begin that way.

This story is sure and true about a young woman that fell too soon. Nevertheless your heart will break when you hear her tell. She is always by your side until her very last day.

Her journey started mid-spring and falling in love was the theme. The weather is warm, the birds flying around in the sky spreading their wings to go higher in the sky, flowers are blooming to show off their color very soon. Walking through the fields wondering where this life will fulfill.

As she flashbacks through the years when everything seems to disappear from view but something just revolves around you, lingering thoughts of memories that play with her mind, pretending to always be mine. You gave her a look that shook her soul and never wanted to leave you alone. That's the day when she fell for you , wondering why she's still with you.

Another flash comes to play, she remembers the taste of your lips, the flavor of tongue that tastes like bubblegum, feeling your touch bring her to pleasure of joy that's why you was her favorite. Her mind spins to full happiness and sadness, your bad boy role comes with a toll, wearing her spirit down leaving her feeling like a clown. You didn't care to see the damage you left within her, leaving her to suffer with no more Love to share. The heartbreak he gave brought her down, loneliness came to play without no one to cherish the love she once had feeling like she wanted to pass, things that she held dear had no meaning because he wasn't near. The frown on her face will not go away because of all the love he took away, no more smiles or joy just emptiness she felt and wanted the desire to melt. Spring has come again bringing her feelings for him to an End.

This is where we begin with another tale about someone falling in love again like a fool. This is a Journey we will all take with different people,time,place or world; everything in this timeline swirls.

Her body starts flowing in the air bringing her heart, mind and soul all together. The lightest of her spirit is free to explore everything inside of herself to mature. To be reborn is the greatest pleasure to always find who's your treasure.

Her soul is pure with a heart and mind that is clear to start another journey without any fears for a new life to appear.

Back Story

This poem is about change from one life to another, letting go of the past so you can have faith in the present and brighter future. Once you release the hurt and pain that cause you so much misery in life then that's when you free yourself. Let go… so your new journey in life can begin.

SERVE AND PROTECT

Law and Order so they say; playing with people lives everyday. Having no Respect for upholding the law just going around withholding your own justice in dismay.

No accountability for your stance, not giving no one a chance.

Serve and Protect that's a joke shooting and killing that's all you know doesn't matter who they were, you just laid them down like a deck of cards you threw on the floor. The lives you take are never a mistake trying to live in this world is like a chess game ; hoping your strategy won't lead you wrong and you get to go home. Begin misunderstood we were raised in hood and everyone thinks we're no good.

If you take time to learn more about the neighborhood you are supposed to Protect and Serve, instead you focus on what you can detect the imperfect balance of a person's intellect so you suspect the worst from a person that you suppose to protect.

Serve and Protect just like you do your own, uphold the law and order for everyone, don't pick and choose because you will lose. Know the difference between the people that need you to Protect and Serve them.

Back Story

This poem is about upholding the law and following the rules, not picking and choosing on who to protect and serve. This job is hard and it's built on trust but without all the underhand BS, I know that officers are in danger everyday and they do put their lives on the line and I am grateful for that, but some go too far and are not held accountable for their actions. NOT all COPS are bad apples. Just remember to take care of your neighborhood and they will take care of you.

You Don't Care

You don't care about anything that doesn't affect you. As long as you have your money, houses, cars, jewelry, something material you are good.

Greed is your best friend and lover, unless when everything is discover, nothing else matters on how you live your life, you use others in your savage sacrifice. You don't care if people are struggling to live or even how they will pay a bill, the starving and the homeless have nowhere to go, sleeping on the street trying to stay warm, sitting on the curb because you kicked them out of their homes.

As long as you know that this isn't you, you're just laughing and joking on someone else's downfall because right now you have it all. In this class you belong to making people's lives difficult and confused. The people you're suppose to help is the needy, but instead you became greedy with you're scheming from the top, middle and bottom while leaving behind nothing.

You don't care about the way you get your wealth; others are dying because of their poor health. You're shameless in the view when people see you, now that you have the world in the palm of your hands you will never understand the struggle of someone that has less than you.

Being born into wealth gives you an advantage over many, you get your pleasure looking down on the ones that had to work for want you were given. One day you will be spinned around in your lies and deceit, while digging holes with spikes that you had once disguised.

You will never know the struggle of someone who has been through so much, this will make you feel out of touch, the hurt and pain while screaming in the rain wondering if you ever have enough to fill you up. Having your wealth is all you know, maybe one day you will see this trap that you put in place for me will turn on its head and you will be the one that turns into me.

Back Story

Just writing what I was feeling on things that were happening in the world. I pray that everything will turn around for the best.

N-WORD

There's a word that has been used for so long that it's running out of gas, only in simple times this word would have passed. Back in the day this word was used to degrade or disrespect a person of color but now we're fast forwarding today where this word should stay in the past.

This word(Nigga) has no power over me, I'm not bonded in nature as you shall see, this word doesn't control me as you thought it would. I laugh at you because you're mad that it doesn't affect me like it should.

As today timeline, in the black community the word is a greeting but to the KKK it's a meeting.

A simple mind will always try to destroy someone to make themselves feel superior, this is a new era—think before you speak. When you use this negative word in vain, you yourself become that word, your character is the definition of the word you speak to describe another race that's passing you at a smooth pace. When you think you're going to get a reaction from me I'll let it reflect you instead of me.

The Ruling has come. I'm more important than you. I (Myself) don't respond to a Peasant that's not worth my time, I'm a Queen/ or King this word is beneath me. I raise as you fall, with disgrace with the rest of your race.

So remember when you use this word so much it loses its value and it has no meaning. Hating someone for being in a different race is a waste of time that you cannot replace, robbing you of happiness in your life.

BackStory

OKay this might be uncomfortable for some but this is my feelings about this poem, The N-word is basically outdated, it's a negative saying, it's not as effective today as it was back in the day. So my opinion is— Stop saying it because you're more of the N-word than the person you're saying it to.

TAINTED

The power that you have gained should be used to help not for destruction and pain.

You want others to fight the battles you yourself will never join, you want to send other people's sons, daughters, mothers and fathers to die for your cause. You stand in front of the crowds making empty promises to make them smile and saying things not true, once you get the job the money starts to pour in; you forget about the people that voted you in.

Making dark alley arrangements, bribing to keep you in power, never really caring about the life you destroy with cowardice and greed, paying for your shit that will never end with all your deceit.

You destroy everything you touch; drowning in innocent blood for a battle that wasn't theirs to touch, turning a blind eye you didn't care about the people that were living there.

The wealthy get richer with every signal body that falls,while the others don't stand at all.

Middle class and the poor always get kicked in the ass with no ending sore, while fat cats pockets get full from lies with a deranged person holding a sword.

Morals of family values that's a laugh, that is dropping down in the dirty drain while rape victims crying in the rain, Serve and Protect has gone out the window and has no value, power tripping is the new theme they just brush it off as a scheme, Karen's and Ken's need to be trolled because they are a part of the issues in whole.

Crying with crocodile tears working their privilege with all your peers, getting away with murder that you have committed on the street, being praised as a hero so to speak, pleaing forgiveness that's funny to me. I will never understand the world of shit leaving US good people to clean out the ditch.

The people are waking to your game, they're not asleep that you once claim, the clarity of the truth is coming into the light, the vile that had all your secrets is losing the darkness giving US a view to the BS you were talking. Your scheming, conning and lies are being revealed some of y'all are going to squeal. Using and abusing the power you have makes you look powerless, pointless and sad, you do anything to make the people mad. They already burst into your Kingdom that you thought you were safe, rumbling through the halls not having any respect at all, going in your office with a grin looking at papers that you have all your secrets in. They're climbing the walls, breaking the widows to get inside and you were trying to run and hide. You appoint yourself a Ruler of all not being tested by no one when they fall. The same way you gain your power, you will cancel yourself out within an hour, what is done in the dark will shine brightly in the light. Remember that statement when you're alone at night.

The world is changing to correct the history that has been stolen because the Present and Future is coming to play and they will put your ass on display, show everyone your life like a movie, putting on a loop so everyone will know your story.

Do good by the PEOPLE and they shall treat you the same no shortcuts through life or it will repeat the same.

BackStory

This poem is about how the world is going the way that it is. We can do better. We can say something to change the way RICH people are doing the middle and lower class so badly. We have a voice to scream and yell to be heard, fighting for what's right for other people to survive in this world. Outdated people shouldn't have so much power over millions of people that don't do the job they were appointed to by the people. They are supposed to work for us, not us working for them. Think about that.

Your Decision(s)

You hate someone for the color of their skin. The soul can't help which body it jumped into, wasting your time on so much hate you need to go recuperate. Shaming a person for their cultural rights, sneaking around like a thief in the night, easing the writing in the sand while holding a knife in your left hand.

Making up stories to make you look like a hero but underneath you nothing but a zero. All your hand talk is nothing but a muse, you're really nothing but a joker that's dazed and confused.

I'm canceling your subscription, I almost forgot to mention, your logic is unproven, that's why you're losing. Your character and mind is running out of time. The day will come when you have to face judgment for your crimes.

The world has faced so much. Let's just get up and change the things that we can, because some things are getting out of hand, I breathe just like you so why isn't that not good enough for you? The color of my skin is non-importance, how you feel and think with your heart and mind will keep us apart during this crazy time. I don't judge a person by their skin, I judge a person by the soul within.

Color is nothing until you make a scene calling me names seems to be the theme, you're not comfortable within yourself so you attack me to anoint yourself, you see there's nothing you can do I will overcome, but the Hate in you will surely come.

My culture was taking from me but I'm learning as you can see, the fact is that you can not handle the means that I display by reading your history with dismay, you took the lives of other hoping that it wouldn't be discovered, my history is Golden you'll never be the one beholden.

It's your decision to look closer more than the surface because my History will remain the purest which isn't all that insane.

Back Story

This poem is my opinion of some parts of my understanding of history and what I was taught in school. Some people will disagree but that is your Decision to do so. But this is my experiences in life and what I have seen through my life, reading and doing research is my thing and some of the history that I have seen or heard from people that lived in the eras when things were so pretty and bright. This poem is written out of Respect not Disrespect.

CHANGING FEELINGS

You give me a feeling of something that I can not explain, showing your face is a pain.

Remembering the joy, peace and happiness that I had, now I just live within myself for the love I've lost, not knowing what tomorrow may bring, I hear a distant ring that will forever sing.

Sitting and wondering why the pieces in my life is falling apart and feeling the misery while we're so far. When I speak out and cry your name it turns against me like I'm the blame, no matter how hard I try,the changes I want to make goes unheard like the silence in the deepest lake.

I shall keep trying to push through the haze hoping to escape this crazy maze called life, praying that heaven will bloom like frozen ice, right now I will take it step by step and deal with life as it goes; maybe one day it will turn to gold.

Back Story

I wrote this poem because sometimes life can be changing for the better or not, but we have to push through it; to find our way out of the maze we call life. Never stop moving, Don't give in.

SINCE YOU LEFT

Listening to a melody so sweet and true there's nothing in the world that sounds so unique, the tears in my eyes flow down my face but in this world there's no room for haste.

Moving through the earth seems like I'm floating on cloud nine, breathing in the sweet air not ready to come down from this peaceful place that I found. As the wind brushes my chin I always wonder when I see you again.

Closing my eyes to catch your voice, listening without a choice, soft whisper reaching my ear just wanting you to appear, my heart was heavy when you went away, no other reason for me to stay.

The world is changing in so many ways, but something stays the same. I smile when I hear your name here and there little things that I catch in the air, the sky is not as blue, the stars are not so bright since you've been gone.

But I move forward to see the joy that was once mine. My happiness doesn't come with ease, the pain somehow fades with every step that I make. People grow just as a new day making everything beautiful and bright that shines so pretty in the light. I'm missing your face that always brightens up my space but now I will let you go—because you couldn't stay, thank you for the love and peace. I shall remember you every day and that's the truth. Farewell my love floats free to reach heaven without me.

Back Story

When you miss a love you try to remember the good things and the laughter that you both shared. I really miss all the people that I love, I know they will always be in my heart and this poem is for them.

ESCAPE

The places I want to go and taste the food that's natural, being in a different state, town or countryside makes me want to ride. Smell the sweetness of the air, having no cares feeling the wind on my face and flowing through my hair. Different sceneries comes to play but all I want to do is stay, be free to roam this earth as I may and study all the history on display, climbing a mountain small or high just enough to touch the sky, seeing the ocean wide as the waves go side to side, mysteries islands around the bend wondering if the coast ever ends, little villages standing low hoping that the wind doesn't blow, hiking in the freezing snow "Oh no" that's not where I want to go. Being able to marvel in life itself is a Blessing many don't see, when you come to feel the goodness and wealth of this Amazing planet you share with everyone else that you won't do anything else.

Live and Love share Happiness near and far. Nothing will bring you more joy than the peace you bring to someone else.

Back Story

This poem is about how to enjoy what you have in life, everything that you work hard to accomplish to live the way you want, standing still to enjoy and be happy.

Sandlot

His world is crumbling down every time he looks around the earth is shaking underneath his feet, everything is at its peak.

The damage is done no way out, no matter how much he's trying to take out, trying to repair the mind when his body shuts down, feeling like he's not alive. He's caught in the sandlot that he never knew was there, but all his problems come to front and he just couldn't bear it, this feeling that he has but the sandlot doesn't pass.

Suffering from misery and unhappiness is at play, deep depression he tries to pull himself out of this rut, because its killing everything that he holds dear to his heart, the sand is drowning him with ashes and soot, he's screaming for help no one can hear like his world suddenly seems to be different and everyone has disappeared. He's crawling and bleeding calling her name, but seeing her there doesn't feel the same.

Why does he feel so ashamed when he sees the change within her? He is so blind to the truth within the woman he has chosen that his heart is breaking, never thought this could be true. She's changing his world to the deepest blue, his mind is clouded with pain and hurt that he's drowning inside. He can't understand the lies and deceit from a woman that he once trusted, but now the darkness start to clear he can see the world that he once built has disappeared, after all the turmoil and disappointment has shown him in one night, that he can walk to the light with a better understanding of having a new start. His mind and heart is clear in letting go of the past that wasn't meant to last. He will wake up to a better day starting now that the present will be a brand new him and the future will be bright as well.

BackStory

This is about a man going through so much with the world, depression and relationship issues. Trying to hold onto things that weren't meant for his life but trying to be stable and force things to work out, turns out he was holding on to an illusion of what he thought was good. Now he's back on track seeing his life through clear eyes that he deserves better.

Both side of the Coin

Looking around with new eyes, it seems that I've been hiding from the world. Seeing things differently through a looking glass, feeling some morals that shouldn't pass.

I know people change but some value minds should stay in place. It seems the more you do Negative shows what type of person you are. A Positive person working toward something to help others gets pushed aside, never getting a chance to shine.

Good and Bad runs in circles. It's sat on repeat Good can not live without Bad and Bad can not live without Good. It's a struggle for both sides of the coin is like a see-saw, sometimes it's balanced, other times it tips more on one side or another trying to see who will survive.

Both sides of the coin who will lead the destruction or joy and peace it's up to you to say the least.

Seeing things from both sides can help you in the long run but when you start to make moves that's not good that's when the lines get blurred, seeing both in a gift don't waste it.

Back Story

The reason why I wrote this poem is because I see a lot of people thinking they are doing the right thing but in reality it's a false information that is being spread around, that can hurt many that follow. Just keep seeing things in clear view—looking on both sides of the coin and staying true to yourself.

DreamLand

As I lay down and close my eyes, listening to the world passing by, the sounds of life are like a lullaby of different things moving around.

As I let my mind wander in darkness, I see a light so bright that it blinds your eyes but brings out the happiness and joy to your soul.

DreamLand comes with ease as I hear and feel the soft breeze; the sound of music comes to play whispering a sweet melody my way.

Flowing on a cloud is nice and cool, making my body drool, soft to the touch, pure white with a little bit of spice and delight to me, smiling all through the night as you will see.

Creating a world of your own, letting freedom roam, bright light never gloom, giving me enough room and space to make this beautiful place.

DreamLand of peace, pretty colors to release; this is my creation that I made no one else quite the same.

Making a world where you can relax and escape from the negative loom of the world that you will leave behind when you go to sleep.

This is your dreamland, that much is true, dreaming of lovely things you can do—create a beach with all-black sand, a rainbow of color, or a hunky man, whatever you want you shall have here.

Relax your mind and let it roam. By morning, you will be home.

Backstory

This is for all the dreamers who will create so much in their lives, who will change the world and their life. Dreaming of a different world that you can travel to and explore, not knowing where you may land, the mind is powerful and you can just create a getaway when you need to leave the world behind. So dream on and come to life refreshed.

MERMAID

Feeling a nice breeze I can smell the Ocean air coming in, I hear the crush of the waves taking my painful memories away.

Listening to the Whales sing their songs, calling to nature unknown, there's a tide filled with mystery things that the deep Sea holds, I move with the water as it shakes my soul trying to taste the stories I've never told.

As I'm drawn to the deepness of my Soul I can hear the sea calling within me. I love the Ocean so pretty and blueish green, I can lose myself in it's point of view. I sit on a rock getting splashed by the tide, while the water spreads and opens wide showing off its favor to the world without any despite. As you may know that nature calls me to the sea to release all my misery and hurt for my tears to float away from me into the deep where my stories creep around until it's found again.

My tail moves in the warm water as I look for treasure that never will be discovery, I move through that water under the shadow of night, play with my friends but when dawn comes I swim to the edge and dry legs, I lived free for awhile but still hear the call of the Sea saying my name, I will be back and things will never be the same, the Ocean changes like the wind one day it's calm the next it's a storm but the Sea calls me again I shall return, with more secrets and mysteries of the land untold.

Back Story

This poem is about leaving all your troubles behind just letting go of all your troubles and enjoying one day of pure joy. Relaxing and changing into something else that is not you. Step into your mermaid vibe and release your inner child, play and have fun then go back to the land refreshed.

Just Breathe

As I breathe in and out I'm letting go of things I can not control with the changing times.

As I breathe I'm going to let go of the negative thoughts that clouds my mind and travel in my veins.

As I breathe I'm letting go of the pain and hurt that someone else had caused to cut my heart.

As I breathe in I'm letting others in my place to bring a smile to my face.

As I breathe in I'm feeling the positive energy from within.

As I breathe, letting my lungs fill with my voice of kindness.

Being able to control ourselves is a privilege to understand the technique of breathing.

Breath in and out is what life is all about,

Breathe in and out, don't let life take you out.

Back Story

The poem is about controlling your breathing when life wants to turn you inside out, but when you take a deep breathe and release the negative vibes, then you can move forward and be happy.

Take this Day

Feeling like I'm on cloud 9 flowing carelessly in the sky, the serenity of being free welcomes me.

The wind takes me higher as my wings catch the air, nothing in this world could ever compare.

Soaring through the skies brings me joy and happiness on how well I can fly.

Feeling the warmth of the sun while looking down at everyone having fun. The weather is fine go drink a bottle of wine, listening to the live band while the kids run around and play, and build a sand castles on this beautiful day.

As the day comes to an end, I let my wings rest for a while as the world starts to calm down, a sunset of vibrant color on display setting the mood for all the lovers under this heavenly moon.

From a bird's eye view—take this day to relax and enjoy.

Back Story

This poem is about just enjoying life smelling the roses. The way you feel about just being you will send you to the sky of freedom to just get away and relax—free your mind, watching the sunset on the arisening. Just take a day for you.

THE HOUR GLASS

Looking through the sand of time, wondering if my fate is really mine?

We're running on empty to reach our goals, is it in faith hands that's will be untold? The harvest moon is in sight guiding us halfway through the night.

Brightening our path to show us the greener pasture of truth.

The sand is flooding our thoughts of how long we have to stay on this land, making the best of the dime flowing through the sands of time.

Reminiscing all the things that we want to do, putting them on hold while we all think of something new. The sand is running thin, there's no other rearranging we can not undo, losing the race because we never had any pace to enjoy our greatest space.

As the sand blows our memories in the air where our dreams start to show, the hourglass is still at bay and the stories are unfolding as the sand flows slowly.

Hour Glass is the key to have it holds all our mysteries in one hand.

Back Story

This poem is about how much time we waste on negative energy. So instead of holding on bad vibes remember the good times that you had with friends and family, don't waste your time on the lost things there's always something better coming from our dreams.

HER SECRETS

As he lays her down to sleep these are the secrets he has to keep.

When she's awake everything is all good but when she's asleep things start to dwell, everything isn't so well.

Her mind keeps going with nightmares that never shuts down, everything from her past came full blast, replaying the same theme that she starts to toss and turn, yelling and screaming trying to get off this roller coaster ride that's picking up steam as she dreams.

The wheel of fortune starts to play he knows that she can not stay, as he watches her wondering if he will ever learn, knowing that her past was rough, it's so hard for her to discuss, while he holds her close to bring her back to life letting her feel him near so she knows there's nothing to fear.

Nightmares come to her at night leaving their scars visible in light, but he is there to rescue her from the dark shadows in the mist of night, being her shiny knight is the role he will play in loving his beautiful queen. Her Secrets will always have their share but she knows he will always care.

Back Story

This poem is for all the ladies that have their Kings staying with them even with their worst dreams. Everyone needs a person to hold them down and understand that life will haunt them and leave scars but it takes a strong man or woman to help them through the rough patches in life. So I wrote this as a reminder we all have someone special that will always care for us.

Water Fountain

We drink from the same tap but everything isn't always the same.

The more you drink in the more knowledge you seek, people have different ways of using what they know, sometimes things change like snow, first light then hard can't really see too far. Drinking a little won't fill your head, the more you thirst for information on life, it seems the cup is not yet full of who you are or who you want to be. The mind is craving the knowledge you seek to know past history is a treat so keep your cup half full because the more you know the farther you'll grow. Make sure you seek knowledge like you should and it will keep the mind good.

Drinking the same tap doesn't mean you have the same capabilities like the ones before you, the tap is different in many stages while getting bolder and stronger as it ages doesn't mean we read from the same pages.

Let the water fill your Soul from the stories that have never been told, letting the water sink in you won't know when it ends, seeking the knowledge and truth has always been within you.

Drinking from the tap doesn't matter where you lay, many have traveled around the world to explore the natural habits of different cultures to understand the grounds on which we stand. Knowledge is the power that everyone holds; Respect it. Learn from it you can go so far in life.

Back Story

This poem is about learning and growing to be who you want to be. The more you know the more you grow. Don't waste your knowledge on life, use what you can to survive and make your happiness wherever you are in the world.

CHANGING

Blooming in the sun how warm I've become. Simply amazing when I'm not feeling blue.

The clouds in the sky are moving in slow motion, you can create anything if you just look closer.

Flowers blooming sending out a beautiful smell of freshness in the air, bird's are flying around trying to find their love fluttering in the sky.

The grass is greener and the trees give me shade to hide me from the rain, that sprinkle down to wash away the haziness of minds.

Nature is showing off her beauty, see how much she has changed all over the world.

Happiness and joy has come back around; giving us a chance to turn things around. Take a lesson and learn from the past, that everything negative never lasts. Changing in nature is restored with positive energy to the soul, letting go is good for the body as a whole.

Change is good, try it out.

Back Story

This poem is about how nature can overcome and heal itself, just like we can; it will take time to restore nature to its glory, sit down and soak it in, Nature is about to show you the gold and silver within.

WISHING ON A STAR

Sitting here waiting on a star to make a wish for a life I want to live. Searching through the crowd wondering why it's not that loud, pacing in space trying to find my own place.

Reaching for a dream that I can't tame but nothing else seems or feels the same.

Wishing on a star hoping that I can go so far deep in my mind, I will not fail never knowing how my mind is so frail.

The trails that lead me back to the beginning where it all began, now I can finally understand the reason why I am the way that I am. It's not a secret to me but to others my life is a mystery.

I wish on a Star to take me back to where I was happy and at peace, not realizing how I needed to be released, this journey I can see I was just trying to be the real me.

As this life is about finding who I am and not worrying about who I was. Wishing on a Star.

Back Story

This poem is about letting go of the old self and finding yourself in a positive light, bringing you to somewhat of a full circle but still have room to learn more about yourself. Only remember the way you felt when you were happy and at peace within you and not the world behind you. You wished on a star to remind you where you are today and hopefully return there the next. Well that is what this poem means to me. Hopefully you feel the same.

Loving You

The warmth of the sun on my face, listening to the Ocean rushing against the tides looking out on the wide scales of the sea tail.

Laying down on the sand feeling the wetness between my hands, laughing and relaxing in a way that comes once a day.

Seeing your smile is paradise in my eyes, I want to keep you here for a very long time, just laying there holding your hand without no care in the world, just you and I with pure joy at heart where no one can tear us apart.

Days like these are just a dream, capturing each moment so it seems. Beginning with you is all I need bringing peace and serenity.

An Ocean view and having you there's nothing else compares the Love I have for you.

Loving you is all I need to do and Thank you for Loving me too.

Back Story

This poem is about Love. The Love that you share with someone that you can not ever see yourself without. Your ups, down, sadness and happiness nothing can break you from the Love you share with that special Man or Woman. Keep that Light and shine, your love will always be brighter for all times.

KARMA

First things first if you don't want to be treated nasty and disrespectful check yourself on how you come towards others.

When you show your true colors to people they will treat you accordingly based on your personality that you display, you will not be dismayed.

What you put out unto the world, it comes back (10) times fold, wishing that you never were told for things to unfold.

Treat people like you want to be treated, with kind words and actions. Good Karma will bless you in many ways and negative Karma will come back showing your fate in a different way.

Karma works in mysterious ways you will not ever understand, until your hand is dealt in these difficult days.

Karma will let you know not to play with your future.

Back Story

I wrote this poem because Karma packs a mean punch, you know when or where you mistreat someone it will return to you in an unpleasant way. So, what you put out into the world will come back, be kind and show your best self and you will be great.

Saying you're Sorry Sometimes isn't Enough

You say you're Sorry, but your action speaks louder than your words, Saying you're Sorry doesn't change the deed or hurt that you caused, when you turn around and do the same thing again.

Say what you mean and Mean what you say because at the end of this day your Sorry fades away.

If you don't mean to Apologize from the heart, don't speak of it from the start.

Just saying Sorry doesn't play if you keep repeating it in the same way.

Saying Sorry is an empty feeling, showing me your true feelings.

You're sorry that's the truth, you 've shown me your true self so just keep your Sorry Ass to yourself.

Back Story

Well this poem is for people who always say Sorry when they really don't mean it, saying and showing it, is 2 different things. Just because you say it… Do you really mean it? That's where this poem comes from: the truth of how we abuse a word. When you say you're sorry, mean it from the heart before it slips out your mouth.

History

What's your history? Do you know it well,? Do you believe in all the stories your ancestors tell?

How they stole the land that wasn't theirs, how they killed the people that once lived here.

These are the questions you should ask, to get a better understanding of the past, no one ever tells the truth on how they became rich instead of you. Family bloodlines are rusty and blind trying to replenish the old bones that's crusty and outlined with lies.

We only hear parts of the history, trying to change everything with a mystery, when the digging starts all the old lies fall apart, learning the horror of past history that you're trying to hide from the young that want to know where they came from. Everything comes to the light; when dirt is done in the dark alleyways, you can't hide your past, it will come back and bite you in the ass. No matter how well you think your history is covered, it will always be discovered.

Learn from history don't repeat it

Back Story

I wrote this poem because I see that some history is repeating and it shouldn't, I like reading about different cultures that came from nothing and with hard work they change the situation of their life. We need to understand our history so we won't make the same mistakes. There's always a lesson to be learned in life, never stop learning and listening.

Damaged Heart

A damaged heart and soul is easy to get; slapping someone in the face is never nice to do, the most legit way to embody all the hurt and pain will make tears fall like rain. No matter how hard you try things just never work out leaving you wondering why?.

You start to wonder what's wrong with you, why do men/women treat you the way they do? Why weren't you good enough to be with? These are the questions that linger in the mind when you're alone.

Sometimes, we just don't want to wake up but everyday we open our eyes to see another day, I really don't want to feel this hurt anymore. I just want to end this journey it's not going to change, just get worse as the day flies by, I'll just close my heart and raise my walls that I will rebuild, just go through life without no one hearing or seeing how broken I become, I just want to slip away, no one will know or even care and I'm too afraid to share.

A damaged heart that never heals will doom themselves at any time or at will if they don't let go.

Listen to the stories, don't go down the same path as others have fallen into abyss you might just miss a new love that will walk pass.

A damaged heart must have healing time, protect your heart, handle it with care, once it's damaged its hard to repair because a damaged heart will always find a way to fall apart.

Back Story

I wrote this poem because a lot of people had or have a broken heart and sometimes they feel it's their fault that it happened, it's not your fault you just grew apart.

Everyone in their lifetime will have a damaged heart, but you need to heal and love yourself before you can love someone else. Everything in life starts with self, so if you experience a heart break take your time and heal, there's no rush. Love you first and it will attract the one that is made just for you.

Beautiful Queen

Sparkling smile with a twinkle in her eyes, she wears her crown high with grace without struggle on her face.

The King may rule the land but it's the Queen who rules his kingdom.

He looks towards her for reason and calmness, to help him understand the confusion of his land during chaos of the people at hand.

His Queen soothes his words, calms his world with the stillness of her voice, keeping away his demons that want to roam the earth.

This Beautiful Queen is his light that fills his soul just right, he can fight while keeping his fiends insight. Her kisses are so tender that they can melt the hardness of any man's heart. Giving him the knowledge that would never tear them apart.

His Beautiful Queen rules by his side with a loving touch they can not hide, she will checkmate him in her special way, but the love they share will not be dismayed.

His Beautiful Queen will always have his heart.

Back Story

Everyone has someone by their side that knows everything about you, how to calm you down when you're angry, how to make you smile, laugh out loud and also drives you crazy, they are the ones that know you best, they love you more than the rest.

This goes out to Queens and Kings that are ruling together and loving each other.

PURPLE

I'm a mixture of Heaven and Hell I can always put you under my spell, it depends on you which one you will use I can not tell.

My background is a rarely explored or even used but then the mist will always choose, I'm a mixture of passion and lust with a little bit of innocents that get lost in the dust Red is fire that burns the soul and Blue is cold to the touch. I will grate you a calmer breeze so you won't sneeze, but my temper gets hot I will blow like a volcano.

When these two colors come together bringing me to life, bonded by both, they love me the most, I love my mixture all the different shades of my beautiful masquerade that is my trick to sooth your heart every time we're apart, I make you feel like Royalty that's my rule no one can disturbed my mood. I am Balance and Peace I'm a sweet treat of kindness but also I can be your worst enemy with a devilish smile, I get excited when I go from light to dark calm and bold, Back in History I was rare and unique, everyone wanted me because I was so chic.

They are other colors that is true but I'm the only color that make you feel so brand new.

My statement is clear, I come from a long line of Royalty, nothing in this world can compete with me. I'm strong, independent, honest to the bone, smart, smooth and luscious to the groove and I can be sweet, kind and so divine plus skillful and memorable to your eyes.

I am PURPLE, caring, charming and your serenity that makes you feel like a Queen/ King, my knowledge on life will comfort your soul as your mind take you on a magical stroll.

Next time you need to escape come see me on my Purple lake, we shall swim across the seas to forget about your scene of reality just take this moment and smile.

I am Purple.

Back Story

This poem is about my Favorite color. Many people have said that they also like Purple so this is for all the Purple lovers out there that knows that this color is the best :).

MY PRECIOUS CHILD

The hole in my heart will not heal so fast, I won't be able to face the world because you're no longer here to save my world.

I was there when you came into my life and I wasn't there when you took your life.

My guilt will be with me until my dying day, that day you went away.

I really don't know the story of why, don't know if I could've changed it, but my heart is full of regrets because I didn't get a chance to say good-bye to you.

So I shall sit in my chair and cry because that's all I can do.

I will move forward with you in mind, not one day will go by when my thoughts are not on you.

My Precious Child you wasnt mine but you were my baby that I hope to see, maybe one day we shall meet, laughing, joking around and smiling big when I see you again in Heaven.

Until then, this much is true I love you too moon and back this will be our little pack, the keeping this promise as I speak is to remember you well with a smile to never dwell for your soul I will seek promise I shall keep.

Back Story

This poem is about losing a loved one too soon.

Trying to get pass the hurt of another day without seeing them again, no matter how hard it is we shall see them again. Their journey has ended but a new life has started.

Bless every child here or in heaven.

HEAVENLY ANGEL

My tears are falling from my eyes, the look of sadness I can't disguise. You were my world and now it's crashing down, you are my peace, my safe place to hide, I don't feel like I belong now that you're gone, the feelings inside have lost their shine.

I know that I have to stand my ground. You taught me life lessons everyday since I was born until your last day. The memories of my life are all about you My Heavenly Angel, the laughter, joy and even some tears but I always knew you will always be near. Now it's time to say farewell to my Heavenly Angel that floats around with pure white wings that will always make me smile.

My Heavenly Angel, the mother that GOD had blessed me with for many years of my life. She gained her wings that she earned all her life, flying around keeping the light bright so I can see my way through the night.

She's my mother that I will love until my dying day, I will think of her everyday, for now I'll say my goodbyes until I see you again, so fly high spread your beautiful wings to reach the clouds floating in the skies.

Back Story

This poem was written for a friend of mine who lost her mother to Cancer, I didn't have any advice for her or I didn't know how to comfort her. The only thing that I could do is be a listening ear and shoulder for her to cry. When I wrote this I was thinking of my mother, how I would feel if I lost her.

So I dedicate this poem to her and her mother.

RAINBOW UNITED

Beautiful colors, all different shades for me to see.
All the colors are bright that blinds me with their beauty,
The dark colors are what I love, how they sprinkle in the light.
Learning and teaching each other it feels good like no other.
Have a seat, sit down let's talk about places that we haven't seen or
just chat about anything where can we meet? online or face to
face . It doesn't matter if we have space.
It's good to meet new people, learning their history and culture. It's
all good to me.
Education is free in understanding everyone responsible in the world.
Colors of the Rainbow are strong and true, every single shade is
beautiful to explore.
Rainbow United is simple and blissed you want on this.

Backstory

I wrote this poem because this is our world of different shades of history and the culture that some people still practice today; you can learn so much about a people when you know their history. Some history are not very good, but at least you're trying to learn and understand. I like learning different languages and reading on how it became so important to whomever; it's cool.

This is why I wrote "Rainbow United."

❦✕❦

THE FUTURE

The world is changing so fast, different kind of pace you can have, the young people are coming into their own, shaking up the world like you never knew.

They speak from their hearts, trying to clear the air, stomping their feet, beating on the drums like they don't care, giving ideas to the lost and confused with lessons that weren't being used.

They will fight, argue and discuss issues they don't want to miss they have nothing to lose, trying not to dismiss the change and undo the mistakes this Country has made.

They're The Future that will come to pass, they're taking names and whooping asses.

They're learning and teaching the next generation that if you want to change, you have to make it happen.

Don't sit back and take the punches, learn and explore this Nation

The world is changing, let the young teach you old dogs something new.

It's never too late to educate the young because one day they will run the world.

Backstory

This poem is for the young people of today and tomorrow. They are learning and educating themselves on how the world they want to live in is changing and exploring history, seeking the truth of this nation. Don't stand there teaching them, and you might learn something different.

About the Author

Hello, readers. I'm a first-time author trying to spread positive vibes through good poetry to everyone. I hope that it will bring you joy in your everyday life and taking you to another world with your own imagination. I have a variety of poetry that will make you laugh, cry, think, and feel good, letting you know that everyone has a place in this world—you're not alone. I have written some poems that help me make it to this point of sharing my poetry when I was afraid and only let family and close friends read, but now I want everyone to read, and hopefully, you will enjoy, cuddle up, and relax and let the poetry take you away.